EDGE
BOOKS™

Investigating Unsolved Mysteries

BIGFOOT
AND
YETI

MYTH OR REALITY?

by Mary Colson

CAPSTONE PRESS
a capstone imprint

Edge Books are published by Capstone Press,
1710 Roe Crest Drive, North Mankato, Minnesota 56003
www.capstonepub.com

Library of Congress Cataloging-in-Publication Data
Library of Congress Cataloging-in-Publication data is available on the Library of
Congress website.
ISBN 978-1-5435-3569-3 (library binding)
ISBN 978-1-5435-3573-0 (paperback)
ISBN 978-1-5435-3577-8 (eBook PDF)

Editorial Credits
Mandy Robbins, editor; Kayla Rossow, designer; Morgan Walters, media researcher;
Gene Bentdahl, production specialist

Photo Credits
Alamy: Chronicle, bottom right 21, John Zada, middle 25; Getty Images: Earth
Imaging, bottom left 7, Visual Studies Workshop, top right 7; iStockphoto:
RichVintage, top right 9; Newscom: Crowther Mirrorpix, bottom right 13, Everett
Collection, top right 17, United Archives/IFTN, top right 11; Reuters: Gopal
Chitrakar, bottom right 15; Shutterstock: aleks1949, top right 27, andreiuc88, top
4, top 29, top 30, top 32, Avigator Thailand, background 23, Belozorova Elena,
top left 13, BMJ, background 15, Christian Hinkle, background 19, creativemarc,
(earth) Cover, Daniel Prudek, bottom 23, Dave Nelson, top left 21, Designua, top 23,
Destinyweddingstudio, (footprint) Cover, Everett Historical, middle 19, FWStudio,
(chalk texture) design element throughout, GROGL, background 5, middle 31, Hung
Chung Chih, background 25, Kelly vanDellen, bottom 4, bottom 32, Marten_House, 3,
MH Anderson Photography, 1, MoLarjung, background 17, Nate Derrick, background
11, Oleg Moskaliuk, background 21, back cover, PlusONE, background 28, rlassman,
2, Saulius Damulevicius, background 13, Teri Virbickis, right 5, Vera Larina, (fur)
Cover, www.julian.pictures, background 27, zlikovec, background 7, ZullU InFocus,
background 9

Printed and bound in the USA.   PA017

TABLE OF CONTENTS

Introduction

BIGFOOT AND THE YETI: TWO UNSOLVED MYSTERIES

People tell stories of strange creatures all over the world. In North America some people believe a giant ape called bigfoot lives in the forests. In the mountains of the **Himalayas**, people have seen giant footprints in the snow. They say the footprints belong to a white apelike creature called the yeti.

Take a look at some stories about bigfoot and the yeti. Some people believe these stories really happened. Others do not. Learn about the facts and some famous fakes. Then you can make up your own mind. Do these huge creatures really exist? How can science help solve the mystery?

Himalayas—a mountain range along the border between India and Tibet

Famous Fakes!

Some people spend a lot of time and effort on making footprints, photographs, and even films look real. Some fakes are easier to spot than others. In 1958 huge footprints were found near Bluff Creek in California. How did they get there? What made them? The footprints remained a mystery for more than 40 years. They were finally proven to be fake.

BIG FOOT XING

DUE TO SIGHTINGS IN THE AREA OF A CREATURE RESEMBLING "BIG FOOT" THIS SIGN HAS BEEN POSTED FOR YOUR SAFETY

FACT
Across the Himalayas the word *yeti* means different things. In Nepal it means "that thing." In Tibet it means "magical creature."

CHAPTER 1

ENCOUNTER STORIES

 Some of the most interesting evidence for the existence of bigfoot or the yeti are personal encounter stories. Of course, they're also quite difficult to prove.

The Kidnapping of Albert Ostman

In 1924 young Albert Ostman dreamed of finding gold. He went to Toba Inlet in a **remote** part of Canada. Each night he slept fully dressed. He kept his gun and knife in his sleeping bag for protection against animals.

One night Ostman woke up with a jolt. Something had picked him up and was carrying him off in his sleeping bag! For three hours Ostman was carried, dragged, and bumped across the country. The thing that was carrying him stunk! When Ostman looked out of his bag, he saw a family of four bigfoots. The larger two were around 8 feet (2.4 meters) tall.

Ostman lived with the bigfoots for six days. On the sixth day, Ostman gave the largest bigfoot some tobacco. The bigfoot didn't like it and ran off. Ostman ran toward the woods. He shot at the other bigfoots and scared them away. He fled through the trees and down into the valley until he was safe.

Ostman didn't tell anyone his story for a long time. He was afraid people would think he was crazy. Eventually, on August 20, 1957, Ostman told the police.

Salish Indians enjoy a
meal together in 1938.

Toba Inlet, British Columbia

Toba Inlet →

remote—far away, isolated, or distant

The Shepherd's Daughter

At the same time that the bigfoots took Albert Ostman, something strange happened on the other side of the world. A shepherd named Xu Fudi lived in a village in China. One afternoon she was feeding cattle. Her young daughter played nearby. Suddenly, the little girl screamed. Xu Fudi was shocked to see a giant apelike creature carrying her daughter away. She chased after it with a stick.

Women in the village heard Xu Fudi's cries. They grabbed sticks and brooms and ran to help. The women beat the creature until it dropped the little girl. Xu Fudi's daughter was unhurt. The creature was dead.

The creature had long brown hair. Its eyebrows, ears, and tongue were like a human's. It also had a flat nose and a large chest. The women cut off its hands and feet. They took them back to the village to show other people. They kept them to warn others of the dangerous beast.

Bigfoots are commonly spotted in and around wooded areas.

FACT
In 2003 six people in the Shennongjia Nature Reserve in China reported seeing a bigfoot.

Cabin Attack!

In July 1924 five men were mining in the forests of Washington State. They saw some large footprints on the ground. The prints were about 19 inches (48 centimeters) long. What animal could have made them? The miners couldn't think of any. One night they heard a whistle pierce through the darkness. Strange panting noises were coming closer to their wooden cabin. Then everything went quiet.

A few nights later, a loud thud against the cabin wall woke the men. Then they heard a terrifying howl. The whole building shook. Something was throwing rocks at the cabin! The frightened men peered through cracks in the cabin's wooden walls. Three bigfoots were attacking! One of the creatures climbed onto the roof. The men started shooting guns upward. They hoped to kill the creatures or at least scare them away.

Just before daylight, the attack ended. The bigfoots vanished. When the miners were sure it was safe, they packed up and left.

Can you think of any other large animals the miners could have mistaken for bigfoots that night?

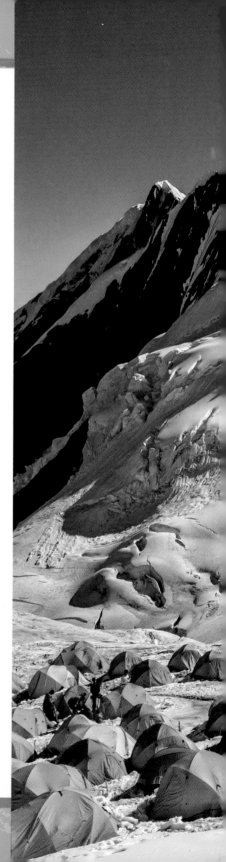

Creatures in the Snow

In 1925 a photographer named N. A. Tombazi was climbing in the Himalayas. He saw something moving on the mountain. It looked just like a human. It was walking on two feet. The figure wasn't wearing any clothes. A little farther on, Tombazi saw some giant footprints in the snow. He took photographs but saw nothing more of the creature.

Don Whillans was climbing in the same area with a local guide in 1970. The sun was setting, so they set up camp on the mountain. As they put up their tent, they heard some strange cries. The guide said they belonged to a yeti.

That night Whillans saw a dark shape moving near his tent. He noticed huge footprints in the snow the next day. Later that evening Whillans saw an apelike creature moving across the snow. He watched it for 20 minutes as it seemed to search for food. Then it disappeared from view. He didn't see the creature again. Could both men have seen the same creature?

What else might N. A. Tombazi and Don Whillans have seen in the mountains?

Don Whillans, 1970

CHAPTER 2

INVESTIGATING BIGFOOT AND THE YETI

Humans have told stories of the yeti and bigfoot for ages. Alexander the Great heard warnings about the yeti in the mountains of north India more than 2,000 years ago.

Today bigfoot sightings are reported every couple of months. Most happen in Oregon. But what evidence is there of these creatures?

In December 2007 a U.S. television crew was filming on Mount Everest. They saw enormous footprints in the snow. Scientists who study human and animal bodies were very interested. They said the footprints could be evidence of a new **species**.

species—a group of living things that can produce young with one another

Look at the Evidence

Can the mysteries of bigfoot and the yeti be solved? Do the stories of strange creatures stand up to scientific investigation?

Look at the stories and the evidence. Then test them with science. This will help you to make up your own mind. Good investigators follow the scientific method when they need to test an idea. This method has a few basic steps:

- Study something closely and ask questions about it.
- Read about what other people think.
- Put together an idea.
- Test the idea with an experiment.
- Look at the results, and come to a conclusion. Was the idea right? Half right? Totally wrong?
- Tell people about the results.
- Think and try again!

Television host Josh Gates shows an impression of the footprints he and his crew found on Mount Everest in 2007.

Under the Microscope

 You can't believe everything you're told. Sometimes you need proof. Just because someone says a hand or foot is from a bigfoot or yeti, it doesn't mean they are. Scientists need to test these items. Only then can we know for sure.

In 1960 Sir Edmund Hillary and Marlin Perkins went to Nepal. Hillary was a climber, and Perkins was a scientist. They were looking for the yeti. Locals gave Hillary and Perkins a scalp they said was from a yeti. The two men took it back to the United States for **DNA** tests. These tests help to build a picture of what something looks like. Every living thing has its own DNA code. Tests can find the code. It can then tell us what family something belongs to. It also tells us other things such as eye or hair color.

DNA—the molecule that carries all of the instructions to make a living thing and keep it working

Yeti Hair?

In 2008 scientists in Oxford, England, studied some so-called yeti hairs. They looked closely at the DNA of the hairs. The hairs were similar to the ones on Sir Edmund Hillary's yeti scalp. The hairs matched the hair of a mountain goat. This proved the hairs were not from a yeti at all. Scientists have also tested other bigfoot hair. The results show that this hair doesn't match any known animal. Using the scientific method, what could this mean?

Man or Beast?

Most reports of bigfoots and yetis say the creatures are tall, hairy, and stinky. Scientists ask questions when a possible new species is discovered. For example, if bigfoots and yetis actually exist, what sort of creature are they? Some scientists think the yeti is a mountain bear. Others think it is a kind of giant ape. In China **fossils** of a giant ape were found. Do you think the yeti could be a bear or a giant ape?

In 1859 scientist Charles Darwin wrote a book. The book explained how Darwin believed humans developed over time. This book changed what many people thought about creation. According to Darwin's scientific theory, humans **evolved** from apes. Today some people believe that bigfoots and yetis could be a kind of **prehistoric** human.

fossil—the remains or traces of plants and animals that are preserved as rock

evolve—for a type of life-form to change over time from one species to another

prehistoric—from a time before history was recorded

Charles Darwin in the late 1800s

FACT
On January 15, 2001, a camper in a Pennsylvania state park was startled awake by awful cries. He peered out of his tent. He saw a tall creature that stank like a skunk.

CHAPTER 3
STUDYING THE EVIDENCE

In Oregon bigfoot hunters have set up special cameras on trees. They are hoping to get photographic evidence of the creature. But can we always trust photographs? Today computers make photo trickery easy. Even in the 1950s and 1960s, it was possible to make good fake pictures.

Many bigfoot and yeti reports are based on people seeing giant footprints. In 1951 Eric Shipton and his team were attempting to climb Mount Everest. They saw huge footprints in the ice. They thought they had found proof of the yeti. They took photographs.

Today scientists still question Shipton's photographs. Is the heel too narrow to be a bear? Are the toes too far apart to be a human? Are there two big toes? Look closely at the photograph. What do you think? Could the prints be real? Could they have been faked? If so, how?

Many scientists think that wind caused the footprints. Wind picks up small snowflakes. It then spreads them over a wide area. When this happens, a bear print could become larger than it originally was.

Cameras attached to trees
are called trail cameras.

Eric Shipton's
mysterious footprint

21

Sound Waves and Thin Air

Many people who say they've seen a bigfoot or yeti report that they have heard strange screams. Is this proof of a new creature? Can the sounds be explained in some other way?

All sounds are made up of waves. When a sound wave meets an obstacle, such as a tree, some of the sound bounces back. The rest gets absorbed by the obstacle. This makes the sound change. Think of someone calling your name through a wall. Then think of someone calling your name across a wide, open space. Are the sounds different? Because of how sound waves work, we sometimes mistake what we are hearing. Perhaps what people think is a bigfoot or a yeti is really a bear, wolf, or even a dog.

Most sightings of the yeti happen high up in the mountains. At 1,000 feet (3,000 m) and higher, there is less oxygen in the air. Having less oxygen can confuse your brain. It becomes more difficult to see and think clearly. Can we trust climbers' tales? Could they be seeing things that aren't really there?

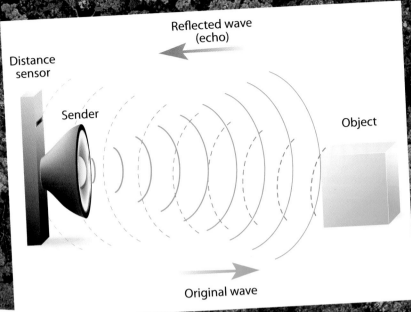

Reflected wave
(echo)

Distance
sensor

Sender

Object

Original wave

Climbers make their way
toward Mount Everest.

Bigfoot Busters!

People are still looking for bigfoot and the yeti. But the search areas are massive. The mountains of the Himalayas are vast. Bigfoots have been reported all over North America. Yet that doesn't stop people from searching.

Famous climber Reinhold Messner spent 12 years looking for evidence of the yeti in the Himalayas. A few times Messner thought he saw a yeti himself. In the end, though, he concluded that what he had seen was a Himalayan brown bear.

In 1967 Roger Patterson and Robert Gimlin said they had filmed a bigfoot. Not everyone believed them. Some people think that the creature walking through the woods was actually a man dressed in an ape suit. Many years later, a costume shop owner said he had sent an ape suit to Roger Patterson in 1967. Another man then said he had worn the ape suit for the film. Do these claims prove the film is a fake? Think about the science and the proof required.

Still images from Patterson
and Gimlin's 1967 film

FACT
All over the world, people have
told stories about mysterious wild
men. In China people are frightened
of the Yeren. In Australia they tell
stories about the Yowie.

CHAPTER 4
CAN THE MYSTERY BE SOLVED?

 Thousands of stories about bigfoots and yetis have been told. Dozens of giant footprints and photographs of strange creatures are real. But there is no proof that these creatures exist—yet. Are we any closer to finding them? Could a human-ape exist?

Some scientists think so. In Russia a team of Russian and American scientists are working together to find proof of the yeti. As the search continues, one thing is certain. If someone finds proof of a bigfoot or a yeti, he or she will be world famous.

In the meantime, what do you think about these creatures? Now that you've looked at the evidence, do you believe they are real or not?

If bigfoot exists, its fur may help it blend in with the forest.

FACT
In Bhutan people believe that yetis can become invisible. Some people also say that yetis have feet that face backward. This is so they can trick people who try to follow them.

SUMMING UP THE SCIENCE

 Two main theories attempt to explain the possible existence of bigfoots and yetis. One follows Charles Darwin's idea of a human-ape (see pages 18 and 19). The other explains the mysterious noises (see pages 22 and 23). Do either of these theories convince you these creatures are real?

Darwin and the Giant Ape Theory

Charles Darwin's studies showed how similar humans and apes are. He also explained how four-footed creatures learned to walk on two feet. The extinct Gigantopithecus proves that, at one point, giant human-like apes walked around on two feet. Putting these two theories together, some people think that bigfoots and yetis could be a kind of prehistoric human. Could they be a missing link between apes and humans?

Sound Waves

All noises create sound waves. If an animal in a forest makes a sound, the sound waves pass through and around many obstacles. The sound waves get longer and shorter as they reflect and bounce off the surface of the trees. Because of this, the sound changes. So what might sound strange is actually just a **distortion** of a common sound.

distortion—when something has been changed so that it is unlike its normal state

TIMELINE

326 BCE   Alexander the Great hears warnings about yetis that
           live in the mountains.

1811 CE   David Thompson finds enormous footprints in the snow in
           Alberta, Canada.

1832   Nepalese villagers record the first sighting of a yeti.

1910   Two miners are found dead in Nahanni Valley, Canada.
           The deaths are blamed on a bigfoot.

1924   A group of miners is attacked in their cabin in Washington State.

1951   Eric Shipton takes photographs of large footprints in the snow
           on Mount Everest.

1957   Albert Ostman claims a family of bigfoots kidnapped him
           in 1924.

1958   Jerry Crew finds large footprints at Bluff Creek, California.

1967   A supposed bigfoot is filmed in Bluff Creek by Roger Patterson
           and Robert Gimlin.

1992   Julian Freeman-Atwood finds giant footprints on a Mongolian
           glacier that no one has climbed for 30 years.

1998   Reinhold Messner finishes his hunt for a yeti after 30 years
           of searching.

2004   Four people report seeing a 7-foot- (2.1-m-) tall creature with
           white hair and red eyes in Chalfont, Pennsylvania.

2007   Researcher Josh Gates and his team find a series of large
           footprints high up in the Himalayan Mountains.

2017   Scientists test hair of supposed yetis from Nepal. The results
           show the hair is from bears commonly found in that country.

GLOSSARY

distortion (diss-TOR-shuhn)—when something has been changed so that it is unlike its normal state

DNA (dee-en-AY)—the molecule that carries all of the instructions to make a living thing and keep it working

evolve (i-VAHLV)—for a type of life-form to change over time from one species to another

fossil (FAH-suhl)—the remains or traces of plants and animals that are preserved as rock

Himalayas (him-uh-LAY-uhz)—a mountain range along the border between India and Tibet; Mount Everest is its highest peak and the highest peak in the world

prehistoric (pree-hi-STOR-ik)—from a time before history was recorded

remote (ri-MOHT)—far away, isolated, or distant

species (SPEE-sheez)—a group of living things that can produce young with one another

READ MORE

Kawa, Katie. *The Legend of Bigfoot.* Famous Legends. New York: Gareth Stevens, 2018.

Murray, Laura K. *Bigfoot.* Are They Real? Mankato, Minn.: Creative Education, 2017.

Omoth, Tyler. *Handbook to Bigfoot, Nessie, and Other Unexplained Creatures.* Paranormal Handbooks. North Mankato, Minn.: Capstone, 2017.

INTERNET SITES

Use FactHound to find Internet sites related to this book.

Visit *www.facthound.com*

Just type in 9781543535693 and go.

Super-cool stuff! Check out projects, games and lots more at
www.capstonekids.com

INDEX